Printed in the United States of America

ISBN: 978-0-578-45965-3

Cover design by Winsome Design
Edited by Michelle Schneider

Printed by Petit Renard Press
www.petitrenardpress.com

# PATHWAYS TO LANGUAGE FLUENCY:

## CHANGING HOW WE THINK ABOUT LANGUAGE IN THE UNITED STATES

By

Elizabeth Porter, NBCT, M.Ed.

*"My 9-year-old says, 'Madame Porter is funny and her class is fun!" As a result of his enjoyment of her teaching method, he is excited about learning French. He does not enjoy learning Spanish however, which we've been learning through a different method. Even though his grandmother understands Spanish better, he does not try to speak in Spanish. He does not hesitate to speak French, even teaching his friends new words he has learned and sharing interesting facts about French culture."*

Ami Vaughan, Homeschool Parent/Teacher

*"In previous French curricula I had struggled with getting a grasp on the pronunciation. Having now tried the method of no translation and being spoken to in French during my classes, my pronunciation has improved greatly, as well as being able to think and speak more fluent French!"*

Sarah Falk, Student

*"Elizabeth Porter's expert ideas on whole language acquisition and communication mirror what our own family has learned through years of trial-and-error language learning. Learning without translation, incorporating all the senses, detaching one's own native language filters from the process, and focusing on cultural awareness truly is a superior way to learn and retain language and to become a responsible global citizen."*

Jennifer Lorz, Homeschool Parent and Language Tutor

*"Elizabeth Porter is uniquely dynamic in the ideas and projects she carries out. She is an essential ally for the influence of multilingualism. Her work and investment are remarkable."*

ZAFIROVIC Nadège, International Relations
CAVILAM - Alliance Française

*"Elizabeth Porter's unique approach to language instruction works ideally or all ages, preschool to adult. My children's French language skills have grown immensely while working with Mrs Porter; they are confident with using French, both in conversation and in writing, and are now looking forward to visiting France next summer. Porter's dedication to language acquisition and global immersion are truly life-changing—she is one consummate professional and woman business leader, and we are so grateful to work with her."*

Anne Tammel, Author and Parent

*"I love speaking French. It feels as though I'm part of a different world, and it sounds more musical than English. I love learning through songs, games, drawing, listening and speaking. Madame Porter makes everything fun so we can join in enthusiastically. I look forward to French class every week! I have stayed in France twice with my family for a holiday, and I can't wait to go again!"*

Avram, Student, Aged 9

## Dedication:

**For Daniel**, for showing me me the path to human connection, for seeing the world in ways that enlighten those around you, for proving that Autism is not something to be feared but celebrated, and for just being unapologetically you.

**For Noah**, mon chou chou, who lights up my life every day with your larger than life personality and curiosity for the world.

*Je vous aime tant.*

*"To have another language is to possess a second soul."*
*Charlemagne*


*"What is essential is invisible to the eye, it is only*
*with the heart that one can see rightly."*
*Antoine de Saint-Exupéry from "The Little Prince"*

# Introduction

Ever since I was a young child, I knew I wanted to be a teacher. When I was in the first or second grade, my parents bought me some old desks from a local school district surplus sale and hung a chalkboard. I would sit my little stuffed animals and dolls up in the desks and pretend to teach them spelling or read them stories. As I grew older, I developed a profound love of language that was fostered by my mother. I remember as a little girl sitting in the car on the way to preschool, my mother speaking French words to me and teaching me to count. I loved spelling and grammar in school the most. I also loved reading, but my real passion was for the mechanics of language, the patterns, understanding how language originated and why it is constructed the way it is.

In college, I studied languages. I majored in French, but I also took Latin and minored in linguistics. I have a French degree called a DEUG, a Bachelor of Arts degree in French and linguistics, a Masters in Elementary Education, and a National Board Teacher Certification in World Languages.

I began my early career teaching English in France to elementary and middle school-aged students. When I moved back to the United States in 2002, I started teaching in an elementary French immersion School in the Seattle area. I then met my husband, who was in the Navy at the time, and moved to where he was stationed. I got a job as a French teacher at the local high school.

Travel was also a major part of my upbringing. I experienced different cultures, ways of life, and met people from all over the world. It was a gift that I will value over all else in my life. These experiences made me who I am today and made it possible for me to share my lifetime of experiences with you. This is my ultimate teaching moment, the moment I am able to share my passion and life-long love with the world. All these events in my life shaped this moment so that I can bring light upon the subject of language, what it is, and why it is so important.

The point of this book is to help change our thinking around language, how it helps us relate to others, and think differently about the methods by which we learn new languages. In addition, I have this dream to create a more peaceful world, one language learner at a time. My hope is that this book will inspire at least one person to learn a new language and create a new connection in the world.

# Chapter 1

# What is Language?

*"Learning a language is to understand*
*others; to form connections."*
*Unknown*

*"Without language, one cannot talk to people and understand*
*them; one cannot share their hopes and aspirations, grasp*
*their history, appreciate their poetry, or savor their songs."*
*Nelson Mandela*

## A New Way to think about Language

There is this notion in the United States that it is not important to learn languages. Learning a language is a box we are required to check off for graduation requirements, or playing a game on an app for ten minutes per day is sufficient for language proficiency. I believe culture in America around language is lacking a basic and fundamental understanding of what language is, and how human brains acquire it from the beginning of life.

When I began my teaching career nearly twenty years ago, I did not realize how deeply rooted language is in human experience. I was a good teacher, but I taught with the same translation methods that have become the norm in language classrooms.

In 2007 I attended a teacher training in France at the school that would later become my school's immersion partner- CAVILAM. CAVILAM stands for *Centre d'Approches Vivantes des Langues et des Médias*; it focuses on teaching French language in a dynamic and interactive way that engages the senses. CAVILAM's method is highly effective. Teachers who have the privilege of going there to train come back with an arsenal of resources and revolutionary teaching materials. I spent three weeks at CAVILAM in their intensive teacher training. It was unlike any other professional development I had ever experienced. In fact, it was unlike anything I had ever experienced in all of my teacher education.

CAVILAM touted a method that did not involve translation. Instead it integrated culture, and promoted human connection, although at the time I did not realize how all the moving parts made up this incredible and highly effective method for teaching language. I returned to school after the summer break energized, ready to engage fully with my students. I had also recently been promoted to the district World Language Specialist and was excited to share my newfound knowledge with my colleagues.

Then my world completely changed. Halfway through the year I became pregnant with my oldest son Daniel. I was having severe complications from the beginning and at six weeks pregnant I was put on bed rest. A student teacher came in to substitute, as French teachers can be hard to find. I spent hours writing lesson plans because I would be out until after Spring break.

When I returned to school 12 weeks later, I found that the student teacher had not followed any of my plans and my students were behind. To make things worse, although I had permission from my doctor to return to work, I was given strict orders to keep my stress low and go straight to bed after school was out every day. I was tired, grumpy, and I completely lost motivation. My stress level was at an all-time high despite warnings from my doctor. On the last day of school, I was 30 weeks pregnant, extremely ill with gestational diabetes and preeclampsia, and swore I would never set foot in another classroom. I was done being a teacher.

Three weeks later my son Daniel was born in 2008 at 33 weeks gestation. My husband had secured a job in Iowa, so we moved from Seattle to Cedar Rapids. I became an instant stay-at-home mom.

Daniel was a tough baby, he cried all the time and I could never figure out how to calm him. At the age of 19 months Daniel was showing signs of delayed development and early Autism. It had been my wish for my children to be bilingual, to speak the language of my heart: French.

In our home, up until this moment, my husband spoke English to Daniel, and I spoke French. Because of the developmental delays Daniel was demonstrating, I made an appointment for him to be seen by a developmental psychiatrist. The doctor told me that much of his delay was due to the fact that I was speaking French to him, and I needed to stop. As a linguist and a language teacher, I knew this doctor was wrong. Normally I would have told the doctor exactly what I thought of his idea, however, I was also a scared first-time mom with a child who was not developing typically. I backed off speaking French to Daniel. I did not stop completely and continued to read him stories in French. A few months later I knew that the doctor was wrong, and I needed to go with my gut. I pulled out that strong-willed, "I am going to do it my way," attitude, and I started speaking French to him again.

By the age of three, Daniel's language proficiency was not emerging as it should. He only had a few words and just after his third birthday he was diagnosed with High Functioning Autism Spectrum Disorder. We began speech therapy in our home five days a week.

As I watched the therapists work with Daniel on speaking and expressing himself, I had a lightbulb moment. Language was not simply words and grammatical structures, it was rooted in human connections. It was the essence of our human experience. Language is how we interact with others and the world around us. The speech therapist was not only teaching my son to speak, she was teaching him how to interact, to communicate his needs, and to make connections. I had a new way of thinking about language, and how these concepts should be applied to second language acquisition.

My next step was watching how the speech therapist was helping Daniel to acquire language. She began with *receptive language* — the language we hear and can understand. She used pictures to help Daniel associate images with words. These pictures are called *Picture Exchange Communication System* or PECS. PECS is a system used to help non-verbal children with Autism communicate through the use of pictures, eventually moving from just pictures, to a mixture of words and pictures, and then just using words. By using these pictures as an initial step in communication, my son was able to initiate communication even if he was not yet able to produce the word. Eventually Daniel was able to associate the pictures with both French and English words, and his language began to emerge.

By the time Daniel was six, his receptive and expressive language skills were at developmental level for his age. My mom instinct, and my "do it my way" attitude in the end, was right. The speech therapist told me that had it not been for Daniel's exposure to a second language, he would not have progressed the way he did with his speech.

As the years went by, I missed teaching. By staying out of the classroom, I was denying myself something that was a part of my identity. I do not feel whole unless I am teaching language. It is my passion. I also realized that all that happened between the time Daniel was born and that moment when he was diagnosed with Autism, was a sign that I was meant to teach again, that I was meant to share my experiences in order to help our nation progress and create a more harmonious world. It is a lofty goal, but we must shift our thinking about language, and the essential purpose of language — to make connections and communicate with others.

# Chapter 2

# If Everyone Speaks English, Why Learn Another Language?

*"With languages you are at home anywhere."*
*Edmund de Waal*

*"He who knows no foreign languages knows nothing of his own."*
*Johann Wolfgang von Goethe*

My mother used to write a Christmas newsletter parody. Instead of boasting about how my brother, Stephen and I got all A's in school, or how Stephen's hockey team won one of their games, she would talk about all of the antics Stephen and I got up to. One year, my mom wrote in the newsletter, "when my children were born, they decided to speak every language except for English! What's up with that!"

It was true, my brother and I always loved languages. My brother and I always took pride in being polyglots and multilingual in a country where we seemed to be the minority. We were happy that we could speak to each other secretly in French so nobody could understand what we were saying. Despite her joke, my mother did everything she could to foster this love in Stephen and me. She made sure we were able to experience language and culture authentically, giving us ample opportunities to travel abroad and connect with the people who spoke our languages. Little did we know how this knowledge of other languages and these experiences would change the functions of our brains in addition to changing the way we experienced the world around us.

Learning a language is not only learning a new way of communication, it can change a person's world, a person's human experience.

## Enhancing Cognitive Ability

Learning another language boosts your brain power. Learning another language helps the brain deal with increased complexity of structures and create new patterns. It has been proven in multiple studies that students who study languages have increased abilities in math and music because the brain is more readily receptive to patterns and logic. Research overwhelmingly shows that bilingual people have two active languages in the brain that work simultaneously.

Bilingual people are able to process words more quickly by activating words in both languages before hearing the entire word being spoken. According to the article written by Viorica Marian and Anthony Stock in the US National Library of Medicine Journal: "When a [bilingual] person hears a word, he or she doesn't hear the word all at once: the sounds arrive in sequential order. Long before the word is finished, the brain's language system begins to guess what the word might be by activating lots of words that match that signal. If you hear 'can,' you will likely activate words like 'candy' and 'candle' as well, at least during the earlier stages of word recognition. For bilingual people, this activation is not limited to a single language; auditory input activates corresponding words *regardless* of the language to which they belong." It is quite natural for a bilingual person to use the word or expression that fits the situation best for him or her, no matter which language.

Recently I was having a terrible week. Every single day of this particular week it seemed like nothing could go right, it was one of those crummy weeks. As I was describing all that had happened to a friend who only spoke English, the only word to describe the way I felt in that particular moment came to me in French. I told her I felt *boulversé*. It was hard to explain to her what I meant, but I knew *boulversé* was the correct word. In English, this word translates to "shaken," but that is not the sense of it in French. It is the feeling of complete and overwhelming sense of emotion that makes you feel like your life has been upturned and uprooted. In that moment, *boulversé* is the word that fit my situation, even if I was speaking English.

I often see this occur for my children, especially my 5-year-old son Noah. Noah will often begin a sentence in one language and finish it in another, or refer to a word in French while speaking English. For example,

Noah often asks, "May I have some *lait s'il vous plait?*" (lait means "milk" in French) or, "Look at that *écureuil* (squirrel), *il mange* (he is eating) the acorns." For a long time Noah refused to speak French in the United States, he would only speak French in France. I would speak French to him and he would respond in English, which is completely normal for children. It does not mean that they are not still benefitting from the second language. Many parents worry about this phenomenon: "Won't my child get confused?" The answer is no, they will not get confused, it is natural for language to emerge this way in bilinguals and multilinguals. The brain will work it out, and people who have two or more languages have more vocabulary to draw from.

## Increased Executive Functioning

In recent years, the benefits of enhanced executive functioning on the bilingual brain has been of great focus in the scientific community. Executive functioning in the brain refers to focus, multitasking, problem solving, and critical thinking. Many linguists and language study experts believe active use of two or more languages exercises the prefrontal cortex, the part of the brain that is in charge of executive functioning. In addition, personality is developed in the prefrontal cortex which can play a role in how flexible a person can be to situations, how extroverted or introverted a person is, and how adaptive people are to certain performance-based tasks. The prefrontal cortex is also the part of the brain that is in charge of risk assessment skills. People who speak more than one language also tend to be more adventurous and willing to take educated risks than those who are monolingual.

When I decided to go with my gut and ignore the doctor and speak French, it helped Daniel progress rather than hinder his development. The stereotype of an Autistic person is that he lives in his own world, he perseverates on certain topics, he is completely mentally inflexible, he is literal, he does not like new experiences, and he is bothered by sensory input. To some degree, that is my Daniel, he does perseverate on certain topics that may not be of interest to anyone but him, he is bothered by certain smells and loud noises, he is literal, but that is where the stereotypes for Daniel end.

Daniel is extremely extroverted and loves to make friends. He loves to socialize and will talk to anyone who will talk to him. Daniel loves to perform, he loves acting, singing, and dancing. Daniel was recently in a play performed all by children with Autism and Daniel was the only one who stood up, performed his song, looked at the audience, and danced his heart out. He loves to be in the spotlight and the center of attention. Daniel sometimes has trouble with flexibility, but he loves to travel and experience new things. He loves new foods and will try anything you put in front of him. Daniel is extremely creative, he loves writing and drawing pictures. He is also very good at science. Both sides of his brain are engaging all the time.

What does all of this have to do with Daniel speaking two languages? I wholeheartedly believe that Daniel would not be as high-functioning as he is without the boost in his executive functioning that he has been given through dual language. There are times that accommodations are needed, just like any person with Autism, however Daniel has overcome so much in his ten years on this earth and I believe it is because language has helped his brain development in ways that could not have been imagined in those early years.

## Improving Memory

The more we engage our senses in the learning process, the more our brain is engaged, and the more likely we are to remember input. Just like our bodies, the brain needs exercise. It has been shown that people who exercise the brain regularly may delay the onset of different types of dementia, including Alzheimer's. A study published in the *Journal of Neurology* by researchers at Nizam's Institute of Medical Sciences in India, concluded that people who speak at least two languages were able to delay three types of dementia, including Alzheimer's by four-and-a-half years. Speaking another language requires a specific type of training in the brain and switching between languages requires a specific type of attention. Switching between languages aids the brain in tuning out external stimuli while becoming more attuned to auditory information.

Both of my children have incredible memories. Daniel remembers events from as early as one year old. Both remember the most minute details of events. From the time Daniel was two, he could remember how to get places, he would be able to give directions on how to go to the park, or how to drive to the library or the swimming pool.

## Increased Ability in the Native Language

People who study foreign languages have a greater understanding of their native languages than monolingual speakers. Many languages are interconnected through *cognates* — words or sounds in one language that are similar and mean the same thing in other languages. Multilingual speakers also have a greater ability to understand grammar and language patterns in their native languages.

English grammar is being taught less and less in the United States Many high school students that I have in class do not know what even the basic parts of speech are, such as nouns, verbs, and adjectives. When students study other languages, they are more likely to understand the parts of speech they have in their own native language, the structure of language. Children who learn another language from a young age tend to have increased literacy skills and enhanced vocabulary due to the greater flexibility of the brain. They exhibit increased flexibility in decoding words by more easily segmenting phonemes, and have greater *phonemic awareness* — ability to hear, manipulate, and identify sounds of a language and differentiate different units of meaning — than monolingual children. Both of my children have scored above grade and developmental levels on the Dynamic Indicators of Basic Early Literacy Skills Test (DIBELS). Even Daniel, who we originally questioned if he would speak at all.

## Increased Empathy, Cultural, and Global Awareness

My bilingualism has become an integral part of my identity, and it is so much more than just being able to speak two languages. Being bilingual has opened the door to many opportunities to connect with other humans. There is a Turkish proverb that says, "One who speaks one language is only one person, but one who speaks two languages is two people." A person who speaks two languages understands others, ideas, and perspectives in a way that a monolingual person cannot.

In addition, a person who speaks two languages may have a different personality when speaking a specific language. Nelson Mandela said, "If you talk to a man in a language he understands, that goes to his head, if you talk to him in his own language, that goes to his heart." When you speak a person's native language, it shows that you recognize him or her as a person and respect his or her culture. It shows that you have made the effort to connect as a human being with that person.

Students who study foreign languages have a greater ability to view the world from different perspectives and more easily understand the viewpoints of others. You will hear me repeat this often in the following chapters: language and culture go hand in hand. Language is not merely words and grammatical structures, but the people who speak it. Language, at its very base, is human connection. Foreign language study also increases the ability in the brain to think differently as different languages build the brain in different ways in order to provide a view of the people and regions who speak the language. It helps the student more deeply understand how to see the world. Stated plainly, language shapes our thinking and awareness that we are not alone.

## Boost in Career Opportunities and Salaries

What is the benefit of speaking another language in terms of the future? Many times, parents are concerned that their children will never use the language they are learning, that it will not help them in their future jobs, so what is the point? Learning another language is critical in today's workforce, whether speaking another language is required for the job or not. Jobs in education, social work, healthcare, tourism, and international business requiring applicants to speak another language are on the rise. However, speaking another language is useful for all jobs. Speaking another language helps employees relate to each other by increasing interpersonal skills, teamwork, communication skills, and project management. In addition, a study out of MIT found that people who speak another language in The United States receive a two to eleven percent higher salary than those who are monolingual.

## Undeniable Evidence

It has been proven over and over again, that brains in bilinguals develop differently, and that there are undeniable benefits to speaking more than one language. These benefits go well beyond just being able to communicate in another language- bilinguals truly do use more of their brains and in different ways than monolinguals.

# Chapter 3

# The Disease of Monolingualism

*"Language is a city to the building of which*
*every human being brought a stone."*
*Ralph Waldo Emerson*

*"In the lives of individuals and societies, language is a*
*factor of greater importance than any other. For the study*
*of language to remain solely the business of a handful of*
*specialists would be a quite unacceptable state of affairs."*
*Saussure*

I cannot count the times adults have said to me, "I took X number of years of X language in high school and cannot remember ANY of it!" There are so many mobile device applications and computer programs that advertise, "Learn languages by listening for ten minutes a day," or, "learn to speak fluently in just 30 days!" or, my favorite, "play this game on this app and you will be speaking like a native!" Why is it that when we have all these "amazing" programs out there for learning language, we in America have among the lowest number of bilingual and multilingual speakers in the world?

A study published in *The Atlantic* magazine in 2015 states that less than one percent of American adults are proficient in a foreign language that they studied in a classroom in the United States. Less than one percent! To compare, a study out of the European Union in 2012 showed that 54 percent of the European population is multilingual, and of that 19 percent are bilingual, 25 percent are trilingual, and ten percent speak four or more languages. In addition, 98 percent of European adults believe that learning another language from elementary school is essential for the future of their children. Why is America falling behind the rest of the world? What can be done to reverse this trajectory?

Traditionally, America has been a nation of immigrants. Yet historically, speaking a language other than English has been considered a weakness instead of a strength. This metaphor of a melting pot was used much of the 19th and 20th centuries where immigrants were encouraged to assimilate and integrate into the more dominant English-speaking culture. People even changed their names from more ethnic sounding names to make them sound more "English." My great grandmother is an excellent example of this phenomenon. She immigrated from Italy as a young girl and by the time she was an adult spoke very little Italian. Speaking Italian, during the early 1900s, would have been seen as a great weakness. Many immigrants lost their native languages.

Until recently, another roadblock to language acquisition has been a physical one. Our location in North America, between two oceans, created a physical barrier to the rest of the world, creating an isolated population of people. Even today, international travel is expensive, and only a small percentage of Americans are passport holders. Although, it is actually less expensive to travel to most other places in the world than it is to travel to Hawaii or Disneyland. In this historical and geographical context, it is not surprising that Americans do not prioritize language as part of the education system.

## Better Late than Never? Not so much

While it is never too late to learn a language, we know that the younger someone begins, the more likely a person is to become bilingual. We also know that the younger one begins, the more receptive the brain is to new language input, and the more likely that individual is to learn more languages in the future. On average, students begin learning language around the age of 14 in America. Study after study has shown that the ideal time to begin learning languages is between birth and eight years old, when our brains are most flexible and sponge-like. By the time an American student begins their first year of studying language at the age 14, European students, on average, are beginning to study their third or fourth languages.

Many Americans argue that Europeans need to learn other languages out of necessity, because they live in closer proximity to one another. I do not buy this argument. Yes, Europeans live on a continent where all their countries combined equal the landmass of the United States and Canada. However, I believe that Europeans truly understand language because they have so many cultures that mix together. America has no lack of mixing cultures, after all, we are the great melting pot I mentioned earlier. The difference is that, in my experience, Europeans embrace their differences rather than encouraging assimilation. Europeans take pride in the nations from which they hail, yet also celebrate the countries around them, the countries with which they share a common land.

There are places in the United States that have begun to embrace the science behind starting languages at a younger age. Pockets of dual language and elementary language programs are popping up little by little. However, funding is a huge issue, and often these programs fold because other programs take priority in the schools. In addition, there is a severe shortage of language teachers in America and finding truly bilingual teachers for these programs is difficult.

In order to make these programs successful, there needs to be funding, and there need to be qualified teachers. These programs would ensure a larger population of bilingual speakers who might eventually teach in these programs in the future, but we need teachers to get these programs off the ground. Many schools in Canada have dual language programs, but Canada is also a country that has two national languages. By the time children in these programs graduate from high school, they are fully bilingual, able to work anywhere in Canada, or in the world for that matter, since French and English are the two most studied languages in the world, according to census data posted by the International Organization of La Francophonie.

## It Starts with a Choice

If language is essential for human connection, then students must have the option to choose which language they want to learn. Many students come to my school because their school does not offer the language they want to learn. I also hear over and over again from parents that they want their children to learn a certain language because they believe it will be more "useful." The truth of the matter is, language starts with a connection and when students have the freedom to choose, they are more likely to make a personal connection to the language and keep learning it.

There is always a reason a person wants to learn a certain language. Maybe it is because of family heritage, or a desire to travel to a certain area of the world. Maybe the reason is as simple as they like the way the language sounds. Whatever the reason, we cannot hinder the desire of others to learn certain languages because we believe that those languages are not useful.

All languages are useful, All languages have the same effects on the brain. When students are allowed to choose, they will often choose to learn more languages in the future because they find the process of learning language an enjoyable experience. The problem lies in the fact that we do not have enough language teachers in the United States as it is, and Spanish is the most dominant secondary language to study, with the greatest number of proficient teachers.

As fewer college students are studying languages and becoming teachers, and less funding goes toward language programs in schools, choices are becoming increasingly limited. I believe this is why so many "learn independently in ten minutes per day" programs are coming to market. This is one of the very reasons I opened my school: students need choices that are better than "learn to speak in just ten minutes per day." They need choices that offer a human connection and an interactive experience. We cannot learn language in a bubble, language acquisition requires interaction.

## Translation vs. Comprehensible Input

Recently, I got into a heated discussion with a well-known second language acquisition expert whose method was revolutionary at the time it was introduced, decades ago. I was walking through the exhibitor hall at a language teacher conference, perusing all the book vendors, latest apps, and language games on display. I was searching for a Japanese curriculum for my school's new Japanese teacher, when I came upon a stand manned by this expert.

In my early career as a teacher, I had read this man's books, taken bits and pieces from his method and integrated it with my own, but then after that last year teaching public school, I put it aside. It was not until I walked by his stand at the conference that I remembered his books and his method. As I perused his new books I saw something that made me shudder. The second I saw it, I closed the book and started to walk away from his stand. Everything in the book was translated. Now you may be asking yourself, "What is wrong with that? Isn't that how we are supposed to learn and understand?" My answer is a resounding no.

As I began to walk away, the man called me back and asked why I was leaving. I explained to him that I do not believe in translation methods, that students will not retain language if they learn it through translation. His response was, "Research shows that the L1 can be useful in the early years of language to help with understanding, and we believe understanding is more important than retaining." I told him again I did not agree, and he asked, "well how do you make your students understand?" My reply was, "two words— Comprehensible Input." He stood dumbfounded and asked me what I meant by that. Comprehensible Input (CI) is a method in which teachers expose learners to language input that can be understood by listeners, despite not understanding all of the words or structures being spoken.

CI was introduced by linguist and educational researcher Stephen Krashen in 1981. I could not believe an expert in second language acquisition theory did not know what I meant by Comprehensible Input. I had heard enough. I told him I did not agree, that research also shows that students who learn language without translation and through comprehensible input are more likely to retain it long-term, and then I walked away.

In my early years as a language teacher, I did teach with translation, I did not know then what I know now. Plain and simple — translation methods do not work. In order for us to become more proficient language learners in America, we must understand that the brain is not wired to learn language through translation. When we set out to learn new languages, a majority do it so that we can communicate effectively in a situation where our native language is not spoken.

Just like our native language helps us get our basic needs met, so does the foreign language. Translation is the process of changing words, phrases, or text from one language to another. Translation is so ineffective because it creates a reliance on the learner's native language to speak the new language and creates dependence on accuracy, hindering fluency. Fluency does not equate to accuracy. Fluency is the rate at which your brain can effectively process and produce language. Translation makes a person focus on every word, getting it right every time, and it takes time to try to figure out how to form each word into a sentence.

When you speak your native language, you hear less than 50 percent of the words being spoken in a conversation. Your brain does not process every word individually but processes input as a unit. A prime example of a translation mistake many French learners make is mixing up phrases that use the verbs *être* (to be) and *avoir* (to have). For this example, I will go against my rule and (badly) translate: In French, we use the verb avoir to express things like, age (*j'ai 18 ans* — I have 18 years), hunger (*j'ai faim* — I have hunger), and discomfort (*j'ai mal au ventre, j'ai mal aux oreilles* — I have bad at the ears, *j'ai froid* — I have cold). English speakers would use the verb "to be" or another verb for these phrases: I am 18 years old, I am hungry, I am cold, I am sick to my stomach. Oftentimes when students translate, they get stuck on using English grammar constructions instead of using constructions in the target language, focusing on every word instead of global meaning. Therefore, translation methods hinder our ability to communicate effectively and authentically.

Translation is a different skillset in the brain. Many people who work as translators are not fluent speakers of the languages they translate. I have a close friend in France who works as a translator. Her native language is French, and she translates English, Spanish, and Portuguese. She can read and write in all four languages, but the only language she can speak is her native language. Translators must be accurate and they must be able to write the language proficiently. I want to be clear, when I say "translator," I am not including language interpreters who must have the skills of a translator and fluency; that is a skill that requires even more specialization. But only a small amount of language learners intend on becoming a translator or an interpreter, most want to learn a language to communicate, plain and simple.

## If Translation is so Ineffective, then why is it the Standard Method in the United States?

A year ago, I was giving a training on my method at a language teacher conference. I had a room full of teachers ready to learn about how I teach language. I prepared a short lesson to demonstrate my method, explaining the reasons behind the activities we were doing along the way. At the end of the session, everyone was smiling, one teacher raised her hand and said that she was excited to go back to her classes and teach the lesson I had just taught to them.

Another teacher timidly raised his hand and said, "This method is amazing, and I would love to have the freedom to teach this way, but in my district, we have to teach to the curriculum, and the curriculum doesn't support this way of teaching." I looked out to a sea of teachers nodding in agreement. The teachers loved my presentation, but one after the other they raised their hands saying that the typical translation method allows them to move faster through the material. Many stated that already they lose significant instructional time with assemblies, half days, and days off from school. It is hard to teach a method that takes more time even if it is more effective.

In many schools across the United States, teachers are bound by the constraints of their districts and lack of funding. There are some school districts that give teachers the freedom to teach the way they see fit, but those districts are few and far between. Many times, administrators are not supportive of language teachers, making it difficult when teachers are trying to build programs. When a teacher faces such constraints, it is no wonder we have a problem with monolingualism in America. The result is adults who took two to four years of a language in high school and never retained any of it. Not only are these challenges coming from above, but we are in an era where students want instant gratification. In order to retain language, we must make our brains work, and yet learners want to know the meaning and they want to know it now. Translation gives the learner that instant gratification of understanding, but only stays in short-term memory and therefore is not reinforced.

Those methods that tout "speak fluently in just ten minutes per day," are entirely translation methods, and they are missing the most essential piece of learning language — human connection. I said earlier we cannot learn language in a bubble, and learning independently, devoid of human contact is rarely, if ever, effective. I believe this idea of learning language through an app in "ten minutes per day" or learning programs that claim that you can become fluent in 30 days are a dangerous premise. These claims are not only false advertising, they are deceptive. Just like you cannot pick up an instrument and instantly play it, you cannot learn a language and instantly speak. If that were true, then all babies would come out fully able to carry on a conversation. Language learning takes a lifetime and even native speakers are continuously learning because language is a living thing, it changes constantly. These programs are also lacking authentic language. Sure, you may learn to say that you have cheese on your nose, but is that something that you really need to communicate? These programs lack the language that people actually speak, the slang, the colloquialisms, the idiomatic expressions, everything that brings language alive.

Another trend I see more and more is that you don't need an actual language teacher to learn a language. Yes, this can be true in immersion situations, however, even immersion situations do not necessarily teach all of the competencies needed to become truly bilingual. True bilinguals can listen to language, speak fluently, read, and write.

I hear many people who say that they hired a tutor who is a native speaker but not a teacher. Just because you can speak a language does not mean you can teach it. Language teaching is a very specialized field. Just like an engineer cannot necessarily teach engineering, a native speaker is not necessarily equipped with the proper knowledge to teach language. A prime example of this: how many Americans do not know or understand English grammar. Just like learning a foreign language, we must learn how to read and write properly, we have to learn the skills that give us the competencies in our native languages.

In addition, language teachers spend years learning best practices, methods for language acquisition, and attend regular professional development. If a learner is not willing to invest in what it takes to truly become proficient, the student will never progress. Even in immersion situations, the student needs to study the language beyond speaking. My children speak French, but they are studying French to become literate and eventually have the skills to go to school in France. Every summer both of them go to school in France to learn to properly acquire the competencies needed to be fully bilingual.

Effective second language acquisition methods encourage the student to communicate and not be afraid of making a mistake. The actor Bradley Cooper was interviewed on a French television station to promote his movie, *A Star is Born*. Bradley Cooper speaks fluent French. His French is not accurate, he makes a lot of mistakes, but his French is fluent, and his accent is excellent.

When the host of the show asked Bradley how he learned to speak so well, he said he lived six months in Aix-en-Provence during college, to which the host replied, "Yes but if I go to Spain for six months without any previous knowledge of Spanish, I will not come back speaking fluently like you!" Bradley Cooper made a point that I wish all of my students would hear and I want all of you out there to hear: "I don't care if I make mistakes, I know my grammar is terrible, I just want to communicate and connect with people. I just speak."

The moment I saw the clip I screamed, "YES! THIS!" Learners who don't focus on accuracy, who don't focus on making mistakes, whose focus is on making connections and communicating, are successful language learners. Those students achieve fluency. Think about how many Americans speak fluently but not accurately. We cannot let the fear of making a mistake hinder our desire to speak.

The expert I mentioned earlier was not entirely wrong. I do think there is a place for the native language when learning a new language, just not to translate. I believe in using the native language to make word associations, teach students to recognize *cognates* — words that are similar in two languages and mean the same thing, and explain grammar concepts. I also like to use the native language in the early years to explain culture because I want the students to have a deep understanding of the people who speak the language.

It is my goal to speak as much French as possible, even from the early years. Sometimes it does help students to use English as a tool. But a native language should never be a crutch, which is what it becomes when using it to translate. As the students progress, around the third year of study, I eliminate English and my classes become full immersion, but it is essential that they have a foundation first, especially when they are learning language in a classroom rather than living in a place that speaks the language, in total immersion.

# Chapter 4

# Engaging Our Senses

*Before you speak, you must listen, and you*
*must listen a lot without resisting.*
*Steve Kauffman "The Tao of Learning Language"*

*Absorb the language, feel its essence, rhythm, flow.*
*Steve Kauffman "The Tao of Learning Language"*

Three years ago, one week after Christmas, I experienced the scariest moment of my life. Daniel fell sick with a mysterious illness. We took him to the emergency room and he was life-flighted to Seattle Children's Hospital where he would stay until mid-January. I sat in the room day after day with him, praying that the doctors would find out what was wrong with him and make him well.

I do not wish for anyone to have the experience of a critically-ill child, but that single event led me to realizing my dreams. By the grace of God my son recovered. We took a trip to Paris as a family several months later and I decided I was ready to go back to work. Despite swearing off teaching nearly ten years before, I had felt for a long time that part of me was missing.

Over the years as a stay-at-home mom I tried to fill that void by writing a blog, getting involved with different multi-level marketing companies, and volunteering at church, but nothing seemed to fulfill what I felt was missing. I missed teaching language. I missed interacting with students every day. One thing I knew for sure though, I did not want to repeat the situation I was in when I quit teaching. If I was going to go back to teaching, I was going to do it my way. I knew I wanted to teach the way I knew was effective, I knew I wanted to travel with students, and I knew that I would not have the freedom to do these things if I returned to the public school system.

Around this time that I was approaching renewal on my National Board teacher certification. Renewing my National Board, I decided, would be my first step in getting back into the classroom. I had not been in a classroom in nearly ten years, and I wasn't even sure I would be able to find a classroom to do the teaching portion of the renewal. The local high school French teachers were more than accommodating.

I designed a lesson and nervously went to teach a group of students I had never met before. I was sure it was going to be a disaster and I would have to redo the whole lesson. Surprisingly, it went really well. It was like I had never left the classroom, like I never left teaching. That one hour in my colleague's class gave me the confidence I needed to finish my

National Board. I wrote a textbook as part of my project, wrote about my research on how Autistic children acquired language and how I used that to design lessons. I wrote about my travels with students, and my training at CAVILAM. On April 15, 2017, I bit my nails down to the nubs as I submitted my portfolio. It would be six long months of waiting to hear if I passed the renewal.

On November 15, 2017, I logged into my account with the National Board, on the screen in large letters read, "Congratulations NBCT!" I passed. Successfully renewing my National Board certification showed me that I had not lost anything, that I was still a capable teacher. It also proved to me that I was meant to do more than teach, I was meant to realize my dreams, I was meant to lead a language revolution.

## A Method that Works

Working through my National Board renewal helped me reflect upon those countless hours spent with the speech language pathologists who worked with Daniel all those years ago. I began doing more research, pored over articles and journals that spoke about the science of language acquisition. I have never been interested in science, it was one of my weakest subjects in school, but this subject fascinated me. The more I read the more I wanted to know. I wanted to know why our system was failing in learning languages and what evidence I could present to help move forward.

Shortly after I began my research an opportunity to teach French online was presented to me. There was a startup business serving homeschoolers in the San Francisco Bay Area that was looking for teachers to teach live online classes. I had never taught online before and like many, I was hesitant about how effective it might be. Nevertheless I agreed, as I thought it would be a great opportunity to try out my newfound knowledge of language acquisition — a completely translation-free method.

I prepared some lessons. The classes were posted and within a few days both classes were full and had waiting lists. The first day of class I was scared, I did not know how it would go. The students joined the class and I began, I stood up in front of my computer and taught exactly as I would in a regular classroom. The students loved it and were engaged the entire hour. The rest of the semester was a success. The following semester I doubled my classes to four, all were full, all had waiting lists. It had always been in the back of my mind to start my own school After three semesters of successfully teaching online, a little voice inside me kept saying, "Do it! Open an online school!"

I decided to take the plunge, but I wanted to be different than other online programs out there. I wanted to run my online school as if it were a brick and mortar school. I also wanted to teach children and teenagers. I wanted to offer classes starting at three years old, I knew that was when language needed to start. By the fourth semester, two years into teaching online, I had built a student base of people who were inspired by my method. As I taught during those two years, I found online classroom programs and video conferencing software that would facilitate the way I wanted to teach. I added an immersion program with a school in France and I separated from the startup in San Francisco and licensed my school. In one school year, my school went from 30 students to over 200, and this past summer I traveled with my sixth group of students to France. The school was growing, and I believe it was because I created a method that works.

## Mimicking Native Language Acquisition

Earlier I mentioned that translation methods focus the student on accuracy rather than fluency. The method I use and that I have worked hard to design focuses on fluency and communication. This is a concept that many have a hard time understanding at first because many cannot understand how a person can learn a language without translation. My method, Language with the Five Senses, mimics the way our brains acquired our native language, the way our brains are wired to acquire language. Language learners very rarely gain fluency through a translation method because those methods go against the natural order in which our brains process and produce language.

There are four core competencies that define the learning of language — listening, speaking, reading, and writing. I split these into two categories:

- *Receptive Competencies* — Listening and reading.
- *Expressive Competencies* — Speaking and writing.

This reflects two types of fluency, to which I will reference frequently throughout the rest of the book:

- *Receptive Fluency* — The speeds at which the brain can process and understand language. An example of this would be listening to a conversation and being able to understand immediately what is being said, but not necessarily be able to respond in the target language.
- *Expressive Fluency* — The speeds at which the brain can process, then produce language. The best example of this is being able to understand a conversation and spontaneously contribute to the language in the target language.

A strong foundation of the receptive competencies must first be built before the expressive competencies can emerge naturally. This foundation can take two to four years to build, depending on the amount of language input that is received and the frequency of that input. I often hear from parents, "My child is now in his second year of French, and yet he cannot say anything more than introductions, greetings and ordering food!" My response is always the same: the brain will produce language when it is ready, when the foundation has been adequately built.

When it comes to language acquisition, students want that instant gratification of speaking NOW. They want to be handed the meanings and they want to produce as soon as they begin. Just like any skill, you must start with the basics: you must practice, and you have to exercise the brain. When you begin learning math, you do not automatically begin with algebra, you begin with learning the numbers, addition, subtraction, and work your way up. The same applies to language. My method follows a very specific sequence to engage the brain in order to acquire both types of fluency. My courses are taught through thematic units and I follow this process for each new unit of study: we begin with simply listening to the language. Next, we put the language to rhythm. We then add in body movements as we chant chunks of language. We then create projects to apply the language we have learned.

## I Listen

The first step is simply listening to language. When babies are born, they do not come out speaking. They spend at least a year, sometimes two, just listening, babbling, and imitating sounds. After this period, children begin to produce small amounts of language, usually one or two words at a time. Children need at least 300 hours of simply hearing language before they can even begin to produce. According to the Common European

Framework Levels (CEFR), the listening period can be up to 1,000 hours, and it can take up to 4,400 hours for a person to attain bilingual status. The same is true for learning another language. That listening period is essential, and takes an incredible amount of time, especially in non-immersion situations.

To put this in perspective, a student who is learning language in school has about an hour per day of language class for nine months out of the year. If the teacher speaks in the *target language* — the language being learned, for the entire hour, this student is hearing five hours of language per week, which equals about 180 hours per school year. This is the ideal situation but, most language teachers do not spend the entire hour in the target language, and all schools have lost instruction time due to breaks, assemblies, early release days, and the like.

This information is not new. Stephen Krashen describes this as the "Silent Period" in his *Five Stages of Second Language Acquisition*. Many times, this period is misunderstood by parents and teachers alike as an unwillingness to participate, stubbornness, or fear. However, it is a very natural part of the process, it happens in our first language. The brain is wired to acquire language in this manner. When I teach, I do everything I can to facilitate this stage, as it is the most important.

At the very basic level, I encourage students to just listen to language outside of class. I tell them to find popular music in the target language on Spotify or iTunes. With increased technology, and the release of products like the Amazon Echo and Google Home, students can also more readily stream radio stations from other countries. I always suggest watching children's movies in the target language and turning off the subtitles. Turning off the subtitles is important, not only is it translation, but the brain will automatically tune into the language that is familiar and tune out what is unfamiliar. Therefore, when subtitles are turned off, the brain is more likely to engage with the language, helping the learner use contextual clues to understand.

I begin first year classes with how to make the sounds of a language. Each language has very specific sounds and use different muscles in the mouth to produce those sounds. That is why many people have an accent when they speak a language other than their native language. For example, Americans use their whole mouths to produce English. If you watch an American speak, our mouths are wide open and all the muscles in our face and jaw are engaged.

French, on the other hand, is spoken out of the front of the mouth, at the back of the throat, and out the nose. My students think it is funny, but I teach them how to do duck lips before they start speaking. It helps them focus on isolating the muscles at the front of the mouth. We then learn to make the nasal sounds by plugging our noses, and finally I teach them to make the "R" sounds by pretending they are motorcycles and putting a pen in their mouths to isolate the back of the throat. We all have a good laugh, but they remember and can imitate the sounds.

# Le Français Sonore

French sounds are produced differently than English sounds. We also use different muscles in our mouths to speak French. Let's try it!

The French speak out the front of their mouths. Make "duck lips" when you speak French. The "E" sound comes out of the front of your mouth.

Many sounds in French are nasal sounds. This means the sound comes out the nose. Plug your nose while making "duck lips" to practice these sounds.

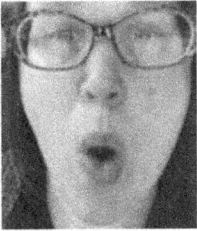

The "O" sound comes from rounding your lips and pushing the sound out the front of your mouth.

B C D G P T V W- my lips are pulled apart and my mouth is closed

f l m n r s z- my lips are pulled apart and my mouth is open

i j y x- my lips are pulled apart and my mouth is wide

e o u q- my lips are round and my mouth is closed

a h k - my lips are pulled back and rounded and my mouth is wide open

The "R" sound is guttural and comes from the back of the throat. Place a pen in your mouth to isolate the back of the throat and practice pronouncing the "r" properly.

## I Use Clues for Understanding

A question I often hear when explaining my method or doing lesson demonstrations is, "Do the students really understand you when you are speaking French?" Yes, but not every word. When learning a language without translation, I teach students a technique that I have developed called *clues for understanding* (CFU). CFU is a type of comprehensible input technique in which students use contextual clues, cognates, and tone of voice to decipher meaning. The technique is to help students realize that they do not need to understand every word being spoken in order to understand the input.

After teaching the first lesson on language sounds and the alphabet, I always teach a lesson on using CFU. It is important that the students realize from the very beginning that they can understand without translation. We start with cognates. I explain to students that sometimes we have what are called *false cognates*, (words that may look like a cognate but mean something different) but if the word looks similar to a word in their native language, it is most likely a cognate.

Students do an exercise where they look at a picture and a word is spoken along with some background noises or a noise that matches the meaning of the word. The student then must identify the picture of the word using the other contextual clues being provided. For preschool and elementary aged students, I adapt this lesson into a song, where students color flashcards containing the words, they listen for the words in the song and hold up the card that corresponds. Students also do an activity where I say the word and ask each student to circle it.

As the students progress through their study, I am constantly referring back to CFU, reminding them to always look for contextual clues when they are looking to understand, whether the language be written, or spoken. I encourage students to listen for tone of voice, body language and gestures, background noises, cognates, and *chunks of language* we have already learned. Chunking is a method in which the teacher gives students vocabulary in context, rather than single words. This helps the students see how the parts of language fit together and helps them with recalling useful language later. This helps when students are using the language in a real-life situation. In later years, when students are doing novel studies or reading books that do not have pictures, they use clues for understanding through cognates and chunks of language they already understand. The students draw pictures of different parts of the book, and vocabulary to aid in decoding and processing the language in the brain, much like what is done in native language.

## I Read

I go to France at least two times per year. When I am there, I visit the local bookstore in Vichy and raid the children's and young adults' sections. The owners of the bookstore called Librairie de France know me now and are always helpful in pointing out books that fit a certain theme, or new releases that are popular amongst the teens in France. I tell stories and read aloud to students as often as possible because reading is an important part of language acquisition.

When I was a public school teacher, I took the time once per week to read aloud to my students. In the early levels I would read picture books, children's stories, and stories that students knew like *Brown Bear, Brown Bear, What do You See?* and *The Cat in the Hat.* In more advanced levels we read books like *The Little Prince* (which happens to be my favorite book of all time), the *Harry Potter Series*, and *Le Petit Nicolas.* Studies show that children who are exposed to reading starting in infancy develop greater language acquisition and literacy skills. Listening to stories stimulates the part of the brain that aids in understanding the meaning of language, building key language and vocabulary. This concept is no different when learning additional languages.

Dr. Beniko Mason, a faculty member at Shitennoji University Junior College in Osaka, Japan, created a method called "Story Listening," based on reading input. The story listening method creates an environment where students listen to language while being given comprehensible input. As the story is being told to students, the teacher is drawing pictures of what is happening in the story and acting the story out, giving the students the input they need to hear the language and understand it.

I believe in the use of stories and reading in second language acquisition. I have dedicated an entire class to story listening. Students simply sit and listen to the story, taking in the language, and building the foundation of receptive language in the brain. Along with reading aloud, I encourage students to read to themselves at least ten minutes per day. As

44

with our native languages, silent reading improves vocabulary and literacy skills in the second language, building a solid foundation for writing in the future. When I was a public school teacher, along with read aloud time once per week, I would also implement *Silent Sustained Reading* (SSR) time. Beginning students would read picture books and children's stories, while intermediate and advanced students were encouraged to read more advanced chapter books.

I also had a lending library, and a program of *graded readers* — which are books that have simplified language based on the student's proficiency level, in French that I would send home for students to read as homework. The graded readers always included a CD of the story, so students could receive listening input and follow along reading the story, identifying the written words with the spoken words. Today, having an online school, I do the same thing. Students are provided stories to listen to and read, and luckily there are now electronic versions of the graded readers I used to use in my brick and mortar classroom.

## I Sing and I Dance

There is a song called "Je Suis une Pizza" by Charlotte Diamond that is used in French classrooms worldwide. It is a silly song, describing the process a pizza goes through, from making the pizza to arriving at your home, delivered by the pizza man. I have used this song countless times in my classroom over my nearly 20 years of teaching. It is an old song, in fact, when my brother was in high school taking French, his teacher used "Je Suis une Pizza" and it is the song he remembers most. My mother, who took language in high school in the 1960s said she does not remember any of the language she learned except the Christmas songs they used to sing in class.

When language is put to music and rhythm, it goes straight into a person's long-term memory. My students laugh at me because I sing all the time in class. I fully admit that I am a tone-deaf, terrible singer, but I sing anyway, and I make my students sing too. At the beginning of every school year, I announce to my students that they will be asked to sing and dance regularly in class, and that I have a reason for my madness.

Students sing or rhyme vocabulary, grammar structures, chunks of language, and silly poems. Students do *jazz chants* — chunks of language chanted to a rhythm, and something I call a *clap snap* — an activity where we take our language and clap and snap it to a rhythm. I make up songs and poems, or I use resources that others have made. My favorites are from Franck Brichet's "DoReMi Languages" and Steven Langlois "DJ DELF" and "Étienne" series. Steven Langlois has some popular grammar songs and tours the world putting on concerts for French language learners.

Music and rhythm are useful tools for several reasons: As I mentioned earlier, language that is put to music or rhythm is more likely to be retained because it goes directly into long-term memory. In addition, people hear language differently when it is put to music and rhythm, which helps with developing a proper accent. Chanting or singing language also promotes fluency, by helping the brain more readily process the language.

Whenever I teach a new concept, we put it to a clap snap in class. Students start out slowly and increase the speed as we clap and snap the input over and over again. This exercise helps the students retain the language and also helps the brain process and produce the language more fluently. The more they practice the clap snap, the easier the language travels from the brain to the mouth. The clap snap also adds a kinesthetic, or hands on aspect to the language. When students put language to movement it is retained and solidified in the long-term memory. For this reason I often have the students act out vocabulary and chunks of language while chanting or singing them. For example, if I am teaching sports, I might have students do an action for the chunk, "je joue au football" while chanting or singing that chunk.

Another activity that students do with music is use flashcards with a song. If the students are learning colors, I might use Franck Brichet's "Le Poisson Rouge" (The Red fish) song. In class, students color each fish on each flashcard a color that appears in the song. When the students hear the color mentioned in the song, they hold up the flashcard that corresponds to that color. This activity engages both the listening skill with a kinesthetic piece engaging the brain to create fluency through processing and responding to language.

Word associations and *mnemonic devices* — techniques a person can use to help them improve their ability to remember important concepts and encode information in the brain, are also ways that students can retain language. When I was 14, my family took a summer road trip. Long hours in the car meant long hours listening to the radio. At that time, cars were not equipped with CD players, and certainly not equipped to stream music. From Seattle to Orlando, I heard a commercial over and over again, "Did you know that if you can spell SOCKS you can speak Spanish? S-O-C-K-S; 'what is that?'" Or something to that effect. I do not speak Spanish well, and years later when I was in Spain, I was trying to figure out what something was on a menu. I pointed to the menu and asked the server, "S-O-C-K-S?" (*¿eso si que es?*). The waiter gave me a funny look and started laughing but was able to understand and answer my question. The phrase really doesn't exist in Spanish, as I would learn later from a Spanish teacher colleague, but it does prove my point: years later, I remembered how to (badly) ask what something was.

I often use word association with my students. In the early 2000s, Washington (WA) State had this campaign to increase tourism to the state. The campaign was called "SAY WA!" (like "say what?" but "say WA." I know, cheesy right?). I thought this campaign was hilarious and when I teach the letter "C" in French, pronounced "say," I teach it by saying "say WA!" Students get it because they know that expression. To teach "B" (pronounced like "bay") I sing a silly little version of "Down by the Bay" that goes like this, "Down by the Bay, I don't know the rest of this song, but it helps us learn Bay, and how to say Bay!" To teach "D" (pronounced like "day") I say, "what day is it today? It's French Day, yay!" "X," is "Eeks I saw a spider!" and on and on. My students think it is funny, but they remember. Numbers are hard in French, too. To teach the number "15" (quinze) I teach "cans of pop" or the number "five" (cinq)- "the boat sank, poor people in the boat." This is an example where I use English as a tool in the early years of study.

## I Draw

Once students have gone through the listening, singing and dancing stages, they come to drawing. Often I do not teach single vocabulary words, but chunks of language. For example, I teach students a structure and how to change that structure. Instead of teaching the word "piano," I teach, "*je joue au piano*," or, "*Bob joue au piano*." The students get a sheet with each word or chunk in a box and we draw pictures of the language. As I am drawing, I am talking to them in French, describing what I am drawing, loading their brains with comprehensible input. The students draw the same pictures with me.

Depending on their level, I might ask the students simple questions: if they like something, if they do something, if they are first or second year. The students might answer in English, and that is okay. In this case English is a tool and they do not have enough receptive language in order to produce spontaneous expressive language — language that is produced without prompting. The correct response in English is not the same as translation. The students didn't translate anything but rather showed that they understood my question.

The next step in this drawing process is doing an activity called *phrases amusantes*. In my brick and mortar classroom I used to do this activity with small whiteboards that students could hold up. Now I do this activity with an app called *Classkick*. Classkick is a web-based computer application that allows me to give students certain tasks and see their responses in real time, like their own personal whiteboards in class. Phrases amusantes is an activity where I write a sentence on the main board in Classkick (or on a whiteboard in a classroom) and students draw a picture of that sentence to show understanding on their own personal Classkick boards . I give the students feedback, if I see that they drew one part of the sentence but not another. For example, if I give the sentence, "The cat ate the pizza," the student only draws a cat and a pizza, I tell the student, "that's awesome! But I need to see that you understand what the cat is doing to the pizza."

As the students progress in their writing ability, I will draw the picture and have them write the sentence. As a further extension, using pictures,

I will tap into my PECS files that I used to use with Daniel. I will create *manipulatives* — usually flashcards with images or words that students can move and manipulate, in Classkick out of the pictures to create sentences. Initially I will say the sentence, have students listen to it, and put the pictures in order. As they progress, I will have them match the pictures to words to see the structure of the sentence. This can easily be done using paper manipulatives as well as in in a brick and mortar classroom. Associating words and chunks of language with pictures makes it possible for students to understand language without translation.

| j' | ai | un | livre | . |

| Tu | as | un | élastique | rouge | . |

## I Play

Young children learn by playing. Fred Rogers said, "Play is often talked about is it were a relief from serious learning. Play is really the work of childhood." The same rings true for people of all ages in the learning process. When a student is having fun, the student is more engaged in the learning process. I integrate games into every lesson. I use well-known language games- Battleship for verb conjugations, language chunks, and vocabulary; dice games; memory games; grammar dice; puzzles; etc.

My students love all sorts of games but their favorite is Quizlet Live. Students love games where they can play in teams and there is a lot of competition. Quizlet Live is a game played online where the students log in and are placed on teams. I move the students into teams by using a feature called "breakout rooms" in my online classroom- in a brick and mortar classroom I would have them move seats to sit together. The students have to answer ten questions that I set up before the other team and if they answer a question wrong, they have to go back to the beginning. The students love this game. I think they would take up the entire class period playing it if they could.

In 2018, I did a TED Talk and I was asked to do a small workshop during one of the breaks between the talks. I decided to teach a short lesson on colors and then have the participants play Quizlet Live. I had a room full of about 100 adults, so I wasn't sure if they would play or not. I was surprised. They loved this game so much, and got so competitive with each other, I couldn't believe it. They kept begging me, "One more round! Please! One more round!" By the end of the break, they were asking if they could play again at the next break. A few weeks later, I got an e-mail from one of the participants that she had so much fun learning the colors in French, she wanted to register her daughter for classes. As Mr. Rogers said in his quote, play is an important part of learning, it is important work.

# I Create

For years I did a project called "Café Day." Café Day was the culmination of our first year thematic unit on café culture in Paris. Students would be divided into groups and create a café. Their cafés had to have a theme, a creative name, a menu, and they would collaborate with the foods lab at the high school to cook all the food that would be served. The students would then set up their cafés in the school cafeteria and we would invite other teachers in the school to bring their classes. The visitors would be asked to visit each café and they would vote on the best café in different categories, and best overall café. Each year, the cafés would become more elaborate and detailed. My students loved this project and it brought many new students into my French program. One year, the local news station even came to Café Day.

My school does not test students, I believe tests are not an adequate measure of a student's learning for language. Instead, students create experiential learning projects for each unit that asks them to apply the language they have been learning. Not only are these projects designed to use the language in the current unit, but also build upon previously learned language. Projects may be as simple as creating a calendar in the first year, to as elaborate as creating a cooking demonstration video in the fourth year. Whatever the project, students have a sense of pride when they have created something they can keep. These projects stick in the memories of the student and because they are based on real-life situations, they come away with language they can actually use.

## What about Grammar?

I am one of those weird people who loves grammar. I find an unnatural amount of joy in sentence mapping. Grammar is important and it is not taught enough in America anymore. Many students tell me after taking my class how much learning French improved their grades in their English classes. Let us face it, English grammar is hard. In English, there is a rule, then an exception to the rule, then an exception to the exception, then an exception to that exception. The French like to think that theirs is the most difficult European language, they take pride in that claim, but it is not, not by a long shot. It is English.

English grammar is significantly more difficult for native speakers and English language learners alike. French grammar in comparison is fairly straightforward and logical. I have heard the same about Spanish and Chinese grammar as well. Grammar goes back to the earlier section on how learning other languages benefits your own. Learning grammar in another language aids in understanding the grammar of native languages. In addition, spoken language is different than written language. Spoken language can be significantly less formal than written and in the later years of language study it is important for students to understand that we are not always supposed to write the way we speak.

It brings me great enjoyment to teach grammar, and I teach it in a way that is engaging for the students. I teach verb conjugations and the different parts of speech, students need to know those things if they are going to continue to more advanced levels of language. The overall goal is to teach the students to communicate effectively and not worry about making mistakes in the language, but that does not mean that we should ignore the patterns and structures that make up the language. Just because the emphasis is on fluency and communication does not mean that the student should not learn grammar. One does not negate the other.

## Mangeons!

The French President Charles de Gaulle said, "How can you govern a country that has 246 varieties of cheese?" Cooking is another part of my courses because food is rich in culture. It is intertwined with national identity, daily life, even the stability of a nation. Food is not only a requirement for human survival, but gives us so many details about a culture and tells us about people. Smell and taste are also strongly linked to memory. Almost every person has a memory about food.

When I was growing up, my grandpa lived with my family. He used to make spaghetti sauce regularly and I can still smell the aroma that would waft through the house, and taste the richness of the sauce on hot noodles. Sometimes I would cook with him, spending time connecting, talking, engaging with each other as we prepared the sauce together. When I teach food units with my students, I ask them to share any memories they have about food and I give them the opportunity to create new memories. Those memories that are created between people are precious gifts that will never be lost. The more we can make connections to the language with the heart, the more likely we are to retain it.

Food is also an source of rich vocabulary and grammar structures. Cooking a recipe, gathering around a table to share a meal, shopping at the grocery store, is all abundant in vocabulary. There are the obvious words for different kinds of food, but what about, "Pass the butter," or, "Put your napkin in your lap when you eat," expressions having to do with the meal itself? Oftentimes around the table, families talk about what happened during the day or future plans. What an amazing source of past tense and future tense.

Following a recipe demonstrates a practical use of the imperative, while shopping at the store is an excellent way to teach interrogatives and the conditional to be polite. My love of grammar is definitely showing now. All of these rich language structures are things that are not normally considered, and I don't want students to be thinking about these all the time either. However, as a language teacher it is my job to think about these things, to help facilitate connections and communications between human beings. I cannot tell you how often I am in a situation and I am thinking about the structures of the language that are being used at that particular moment and how I can use that situation to educate my students.

Food is one of my favorite thematic units to teach because it is so language rich. In every class I teach, we have at least one unit involving food. Food is a theme the student can share with their families, to create memories, and enrich their linguistic experiences.

## Learning from Misunderstandings

In my early years of teaching, I was working in a French American school in the Seattle area. We had a "Secret Santa" gift exchange every December which ended with us giving our last gifts at our annual Christmas party. We had an American teacher who taught English at the school, everyone else was French. The American teacher was the Secret Santa for one of the French teaching assistants who had just announced she was pregnant. At the party, we all opened our last gifts and went around trying to guess the giver.

When the teaching assistant opened her gift, she pulled out a gift certificate to Baskin and Robins and a jar of pickles. She looked up, completely perplexed, she had no idea why she had received such a gift. She did not understand the gift because in France, they do not have the joke about "craving pickles and ice cream." The American teacher was giving this to her to congratulate her, but the French teacher did not understand.

In America, if someone gives you a fruitcake for Christmas, it is kind of taken as an insult; fruitcake is what you give people you don't really like. That same year as the pickles and ice cream incident, some of the French teachers received fruitcakes from American families in the school. It was hilarious to watch them eating the fruitcake and spitting it out. Likewise, the French families whose children attended the school brought fruitcakes for the teachers, not knowing what they symbolized. Many of them thought that because they could find fruitcakes everywhere, that is what everyone liked to get for Christmas.

These are humorous examples of why understanding each other's cultures is important, but it also goes to show that having a deeper understanding of culture helps us connect to each other better.

# Chapter 5

# Creating Global Citizens

*"With languages, you are at home anywhere."*
*Edmund de Waal*

*"A different language is a different vision of life."*
*Federico Fellini*

*"Learn language and you'll avoid war."*
*Arab Proverb*

Three years ago, my husband and I went on our first kid-free vacation since Daniel was born. It was right after Daniel had been released from the hospital and we were both exhausted and in need of a break. We went on a cruise to Central America, visiting Roatan, Honduras, Belize, and Cozumel, Mexico.

Our first stop was in Roatan, an island belonging to Honduras just off the coast. We had booked an excursion to hike through the rainforest and see the Capuchin monkeys. We boarded the bus that would take us up into the high hills of the forest. As we were winding our way through the narrow dirt roads, I found myself watching the people living their lives as we were on vacation. I noticed most of the houses did not have windows or doors, and many people were outside cutting fruit or hanging laundry on lines that were strewn between trees. I watched children playing outside, and chickens running in the street. I was fascinated by the people who lived on this small island. The bus driver told us that only about 20 percent of the island had electricity and all of that was in the resorts on the other side of the island. I longed to get off the bus and be with the people, learn about them, connect with them.

Cruises are wonderful for relaxing, but if I am going to visit other countries, I want to be able to connect with the people and not stay in the tourist areas. All throughout the trip, anyone I met who was a native of the country we were visiting, I would ask about what they ate at home, and did my best to speak Spanish.

Our last stop was in Cozumel, Mexico. We got off the ship, we stopped for lunch in a touristy area. My husband and I ordered some nachos to share and I knew that Mexican people don't really eat nachos, so I asked the waiter, "What is a typical dinner in your home?" He told me that they eat very fresh food. In Cozumel, it might be a piece of grilled fish with some rice. After he left our table, my husband said to me, "Why do you keep asking people what they eat? Why do you keep trying to speak Spanish? Why do you care?" I explained to him that I cared because I was an American visiting their country and I not only wanted to show respect, I wanted to show them that I am actually interested in learning about their culture.

So often when I am traveling, I see people who travel to other countries and do not interact at all with the people and don't try to speak the language. I have heard so many times from people that they do not want to try to speak because, "Everyone speaks English," or, "They will be rude to me if I make mistakes." First, many people around the world speak English, but that is not the point. When you visit someone else's country, it is a sign of respect to interact in a way that recognizes the people who live there. Second, making mistakes is okay. It means that you are trying, and nobody is going to be angry at you for trying. Even the French, as proud of their language as they are, would rather you butcher French than speak English.

A simple, "Hello" in another language can make a world of difference to the people whose country you are visiting. "Hello" is the simplest word out there, and "hello" accompanied by a smile makes a profound connection.

I want to challenge every person reading this book when traveling to say hello in the language of the country you are visiting. In France it is rude to not say, "bonjour." If you do not say "bonjour" when you enter a shop, ask for directions, enter into an elevator, etc. it is insulting. So here is a tip, if you are traveling in France, before you do anything always say, "Bonjour!"

## How to Say "Hello" in Other Languages

| | | | |
|---|---|---|---|
| **French** | Bonjour | **Mandarin** | Ni Hao |
| **Spanish** | Hola | **Cantonese** | Nay Hoh |
| **Portuguese** | Olà | **Arabic** | Marhaba |
| **German** | Hallo or Guten Tag | **Dutch** | Hallo |
| **Italian** | Ciao | **Greek** | Yasou |
| **Hindi** | Namaste | **Hebrew** | Shalom |
| **Persian/Farsi** | Salaam | **Vietnamese** | Xin Chào |
| **Japanese** | Konnichiwa | **Thai** | Sawasdee |
| **Swahili** | Habari | | |

Over the last several years, my goals as a language teacher have shifted from being language-centered to person-centered. I started thinking about what I wanted more than anything for my children. Having a child with Autism, acceptance is key. I do not ever want my child to be bullied or mistreated because he is different. I want more than anything for both of my children to grow up in a world that is peaceful, loving, and accepting of all people. It is my hope that they see themselves as first and foremost citizens of humanity and realize that they are interconnected with every other human on this earth. In finding ways to create this type of education for my own children, it occurred to me that I could make this an integral part of my school.

In April 2018, my school partnered with CAVILAM in Vichy, France, to create a program that focuses on using French to connect humans to each other from all corners of the Earth. This unique program puts language and culture hand in hand, allowing young people to create positive relationships with people from over 100 different nationalities. Each student in this program is an ambassador for his or her country, charged with creating a positive image of the nation and the people from that nation. This is an important role. Each student chosen for this program through my school has accepted this mission, to create a positive image of Americans abroad while learning about other countries to educate others when they return home. As I see it, this is the first step in diplomacy. There is nothing more powerful than our youth changing our world. This is my hope, to create peace in the world one student at a time.

## My Kids are too Young to Travel! Nope, not True

There is a whole movement of people called Worldschoolers. This is a group of people that believe in the importance of *Global Citizenship*

*Education* (GCED) — "A sense of belonging to a broader community and common humanity. It emphasizes political, economic, social, and cultural interdependency and interconnectedness between the local, the national, and the global," as defined by The United Nations Educational, Scientific, and Cultural Organization (UNESCO) headquartered in Paris, France (UNESCO). Some Worldschoolers give up their homes and belongings to travel full-time and homeschool along the way. Some, like my family, have a home-base with children in primary or secondary school, who also Worldschool part time.

The benefits of traveling with children and exposing them to different ways of life are immeasurable. There are many people who argue that they do not want to travel with their children until they are teenagers, traveling with children when they are young is not beneficial because they won't remember or won't understand it. The benefits of traveling with children actually help them develop skills that they will carry throughout their lives.

Traveling with children promotes empathy. When children see different ways of life from a young age, they grow up knowing that other people live in the world, and that their world is larger and more complex than the home. Children are not born hateful or with prejudice, they are taught these things. Children who travel are given social messages that there are all different types of people who live in this world, and we all live in the world together. Therefore, they can form their own viewpoints and opinions at an earlier age.

Children who travel are known to have increased situational flexibility. My son, Daniel, is the perfect example of this. Autistic children, in general, have a very difficult time with changes in plans or being flexible in situations where unexpected things happen. Let's face it, travel is filled with the unexpected: late flights, lost baggage, or getting lost in a big city. Daniel can be quite inflexible on some issues, however, he is better able to handle the unexpected when it arises because he has traveled so much. Daniel has experienced things like late flights and missed trains.

Last summer, we were supposed to go to Belgium after the immersion students left France to return to the United States. I overslept, and we missed our train to Brussels and could not get a seat on the next one. Daniel was disappointed, but we ended up going to visit our friends in Normandy instead. There was no meltdown, no "all is lost" attitude that sometimes emerges when he is being inflexible. Instead he cried a little, told me he was sad, but that Belgium wasn't going anywhere, and we proceeded to have an amazing visit with our friends. When it was time to leave our friends, Daniel said he was glad we missed our train because he got to play with the other boys and that was more fun.

Along with increased flexibility when the unexpected occurs, there is an increase in problem-solving and executive function. When issues arise during travel, a person has to problem-solve to find a solution. We missed our train to Belgium, we had to make a new plan, we had to think through and decide what we were going to do. Any number of things can happen during travel, and each time I have had to think through and find a solution. This type of problem-solving skill will serve a child through his entire life.

One evening when we were in Vichy, we made a plan to go to the beach the next day. The boys were so excited to play at the beach. Daniel had met a friend there the day before and he was hoping his new friend would be there again. The next morning when we woke up it was pouring down rain with a huge thunderstorm. Daniel started to cry because he wanted to go to the beach and see his friend. I told him it would not be possible with the weather, what else could we do? Daniel cried for a few more minutes and thought about it. He decided he wanted to go to the Opera Museum instead. We thought it through, we made a plan, and we went to the Opera Museum. Daniel loved it, he bought a souvenir and was very happy about the plan he made.

## The Power of Travel

There is a difference between going on a trip, and traveling. For me, "going on a trip" is staying in the tourist areas, following a tour group full of Americans, not giving oneself a chance to truly engage in the essence of a country. Traveling is making an effort to experience the culture to its fullest in the time you are allotted. Traveling is making an effort to speak the language, even if you only know a few words, to truly connect with the people, showing a recognition that you are not in your own country, but in theirs. Traveling is a willingness to learn, not being afraid to make mistakes, and the desire for personal growth. Traveling is empowering.

66

Traveling gets us out of our comfort zones, out in to the world where we have to dare to have new experiences and try new things. When you travel and you have to problem solve and communicate with others, it gives you a sense of pride and accomplishment.

My mom recently went to Rome on her own. She had never traveled out of the country by herself before, usually she is with me. She spent nearly a year preparing for this trip. She made arrangements to be taken around to see sights with a local and take a cooking class. She made a great friend in the person who accompanied her to see the sites, teaching her a little Italian along the way. The one thing she told me at the end of her trip was what a wonderful time she had and how empowering it had been for her to travel on her own.

## Personal Growth and Maturity in our Youth

As a language teacher, there is nothing more gratifying than watching your students use the language they have been learning to build positive relationships. Many of the students that participate have never been in an immersive experience before, for some it is their first time out of the country. Upon arrival in France, these students step off the plane jet-lagged and nervous, not sure what to expect. By the end of the first week, these students are settling into their French courses, getting to know their host families, and making friends. By the time they reach the last day of the trip, they often do not want to leave.

One of my 2018 students said to me after she returned that she felt "weird" being back. When I asked her what she meant, she told me that she did not feel like she identified with some of her friends anymore because her viewpoints on certain issues had changed. A few months later I visited her French class and asked her how she was feeling. She told me that she still felt like she had a wider view of the world than some of her friends, but that she had learned from connecting with others that it is okay to have differences and still be friends. That we must respect every person, because he is a human being.

When we connect with other humans through travel, real connections with the culture, we have such growth in our viewpoints. Can you imagine what this world would be like, if everyone had the chance to connect in such a profound way? It is for this reason I want to give every student the opportunity to connect with others across the globe no matter their circumstance.

## Integrating Global Citizenship Education into the Classroom

While travel and interaction with people of other nationalities and cultures is the ideal way to create global citizens, this education should start at home. I make sure to interweave culture into every lesson I teach. It may be that I do a short explanation about how almost everything in France shuts down between noon and two in the afternoon so that families can have lunch together. I also often teach straight culture lessons, showing a music video from a popular French recording artist that fits into our thematic unit, or a short clip from a TV show from Canada.

Culture is an essential part of showing students that real people speak the language they are learning. In addition, there are specific activities that promote GCED that are not language or culture specific. These types of GCED activities help students understand themselves just as much as it educates them about others. Ban Ki-Moon, the UN Secretary General states that, "Global citizenship education gives us a profound understanding that we are tied together as citizens of the global community and that our challenges are interconnected."

Global Citizenship Education is meant to help us understand why we think the way we do and explore how our language and culture shapes our thinking. One of my favorite TED Talks was given by a cognitive scientist named Lera Boroditsky. In her talk, she speaks about how the very words in a language shape the thinking of the people who speak it. In addition, she says, "The beauty of linguistic diversity is that it reveals to us just how flexible the human mind is." Even though our thinking comes from our language and our culture, we have the capability to understand each other, even if we do not always agree. GCED teaches us that disagreement is a part of life and is acceptable, however it is what we do with that disagreement that matters. To facilitate the integration of GCED across the world, UNESCO has identified three core competencies:

- *Cognitive* — To acquire knowledge, understanding and critical thinking about global, regional, national, and local issues and the interconnectedness and interdependency of different countries and populations.

- *Socio-Emotional* — To have a sense of belonging to a common humanity, sharing values and responsibilities, empathy, solidarity, and respect for differences and diversity.
- *Behavioral* — To act effectively and responsibly at local, national, and global levels for a more peaceful and sustainable world.

UNESCO provides a myriad of activities and lessons that teachers and parents can use to integrate GCED. Education should be started in early childhood, even from birth. Integrating books with cultural messages is a great way to start the journey of GCED whether in the home or the classroom. Before any of my students travel to France for our immersion program at CAVILAM, they must complete a course in GCED. GCED helps students learn to think about issues for themselves, form their own opinions, and think critically about situations in their own environments. It also encourages students to understand that disagreement is okay, and to engage in discussions not to necessarily make another person agree but discuss and try to understand each other's viewpoint. When students have a global education, they learn that it is not about "right or wrong" viewpoints, it is about respecting each other as human beings, as part of this world, and engaging in discussions in a way that promotes a mutual respect.

# A World Without Language and Culture

Imagine a world without language and what would happen if humans were not able to connect to each other. In the early years of Daniel's Autism, I had a brief glimpse into this type of world. A world where a person sinks into himself, isolated in his own mind from other people and the world around him. I saw a world where I would never truly know my son, I would never be able to connect with him. That world terrified me because I feared never being able to reach him. I believe that the steps I have taken to promote bilingualism and travel with my children has been what has brought Daniel so far and made him so high-functioning. We still have our challenges, but Daniel is outgoing, friendly, talkative, loves to perform, and be the center of attention, and is more flexible than most people with Autism.

Language and culture are an essential part of the human experience, it is how we connect with others and interact with the world around us. Language helps us get our basic needs met. Language acquisition cannot and will not happen without human interaction, as it is not merely words and grammatical structures but the people who speak it. Language in in every aspect of our essence, it shapes our thinking, our choices, and our very way of life. Throughout the book I have used Daniel as an example and that is because he is the ultimate proof that learning languages and global education benefit every person and every brain. We all have the potential to speak another language fluently, we just have to be willing to change our thinking about language and culture, after all, our world would be so boring if we were all the same.

## How to Use the Next Chapters:

The last two chapters of the book are designed to give ideas and resources for teaching language and culture in your family or in your classroom. These are just a few ideas from the myriad of ideas out there.

# Chapter 6

# Resources

This chapter is simply a list of resources and ideas for families wanting to begin their linguistic and cultural journeys, and for teachers who would like ideas to use in the classroom.

- **Bon Voyage World Language Academy-**
  - **- Language classes, Global Citizenship Education and CAVILAM Immersion Program**
  - **- World Language and Culture Resources for teachers, parents, and families**
  - o www.bvwla.com
  - o (509) 942-8015
- **Steven Langlois- Étienne/DJ DELF-**
  - o www.educorock.com
- **Franck Brichet- DoReMi Languages**
  - o www.doremilanguages.com
- **UNESCO Global Citizenship Education Resources-**
  - o http://unesdoc.unesco.org/images/0023/002329/232993e.pdf
- **The EdChange Project - Cultural Awareness Activities**
  - o www.edchange.org
- **CAVILAM/TV5 Monde Free Resources for Teachers**
  - o www.enseigner.tv
  - o www.leplaisirdapprendre.com
- **CAVILAM/TV5 Monde Free Resources for French Language Learners**
  - o www.apprendre.tv

## Suggested TED Talks:

All of these TED Talks can be found on the TED and TEDx YouTube Channels.

- "Language with the 5 Senses"- Elizabeth Porter
- "What does it mean to be a Global Citizen?"- Hugh Evans
- "How Language Shapes the Way We Think"- Lera Boroditsky
- "How Culture Drives Behaviors"- Julien S. Bourrelle
- "Why Cultural Diversity Matters"- Michael Gavin

## Reading Suggestions for Global Citizenship Education:

These are book suggestions for introducing Global Citizenship Education into your home and/or classroom.

- *What does it mean to be Global by Rana DiOrio* – This book can be purchased in several different languages. I love this book for introducing the concept of Global Citizenship to children but use this book often with my adolescent learners as well.
- *Growing up Global- Raising Children to Be at Home in the World* by Homa Sabet Tavangar – An excellent resource giving parents and teachers ideas on how to integrate Global Citizenship Education into the home and classroom. One of my favorites!
- *The Global Education Toolkit for Elementary Learners* by Homa Sabet Tavanger and Becky Mladic-Morales – This book is excellent for elementary school teachers. Ideas in this book can also easily be adapted and used for older learners and the foreign language classroom as well. This book provides specific lessons and activities that are ready to use in the classroom.

## Books with Cultural and Human Connection Messages

- *The Little Prince* by Antoine de Saint-Exupéry- Every person in this world should read this book at least once in his or her lifetime. The Little Prince is the 6th most translated book in the world. I have read this book thousands of times and studied it with students. The message is about connecting with others, love, peace, and innocence.
- *The Colors of Us* by Karen Katz
- *Wonder* by R.J. Palacio

- *Chrysanthemum* by Kevin Henkes
- *Rickshaw Girl* by Mitali Perkins
- *26 Fairmont Avenue* by Tomie DePaola
- *Pink is for Boys* by Robb Pearlman
- *Esperanza Rising* by Pam Munoz Ryan
- *Number the Stars* by Lois Lowry
- *Night* by Elie Wiesel
- *Kaffir Boy* by Mark Mathabane
- *Habibi* by Naomi Shihab Nye

## Reading Suggestions for Language Learners:

Many of these suggestions will be in French, but equivalents can be found in every language. These books can be used for reading aloud or for silent sustained reading (SSR). "Read aloud" should always be at least one level above the student's current acquisition level. Books with titles in English are meant to be read in the target language and can be found in many different languages. These are just examples and meant to give ideas of the types of books that are good for each level of language acquisition.

**Important note** — I do not suggest bilingual books as the brain will focus on the familiar language and ignore the new language. It is always best when reading with language learners to read solely in the target language. Reading bilingual books will hinder the acquisition process.

## *Lire en Français Facile Graded French Readers* from Hachette FLE
- Levels A1 (1st year) to B2 (4th year)
- Best for SSR
  - o www.hachettefle.fr

## Book suggestions for levels A1/A2 (1st and 2nd year)
- Graded readers in the target language for SSR- ideally with the story also available on audio for listening and reading connections in the brain.
- Board books designed for ages 1-5 years old- even for adults, as language learners start at the very basic levels of language.
- *Histoire de Babar* (The Story of Babar) by Jean de Brunhoff
- *Simplified Fairy Tales with Pictures* – French publisher, Père Castor, makes some Mini Classics that are excellent for read aloud at the

A1 level and SSR starting at the A2 level.
- *The Histoire de Parler Series* by Bayard Jeunesse
- *Mes Années Pourquoi Series* by Milan
- *Doctor Seuss Books* by Dr. Seuss
- *Guess How Much I Love You* by Sam McBratney
- *The Giving Tree* by Shel Silverstein
- *The Very Hungry Caterpillar* by Eric Carle
- *Brown Bear, Brown Bear, What do you See?* by Eric Carle
- *Goodnight Moon* by Margaret Wise Brown

## Book suggestions for levels B1/B2 (3rd and 4th year)

- Graded readers in the target language for SSR — ideally with the story also available on audio for listening and reading connections in the brain.
- Comic books like *Astérix* by Albert Uderzo, René Goscinny, Jean-Yves Ferri and *Tintin* by Georges Remi (under his pen name, Hergé)
- *Le Petit Nicolas Series* by Jean-Jacques Sempé and René Goscinny (under the pseudonym Agostini)
- *Les Fables de la Fontaine* by Jean de La Fontaine
- *Harry Potter Series* by J.K. Rowling
- *Le Petit Prince* by Antoine de Saint Exupéry
- *Arsène Lupin* - Maurice Leblanc
- *Le Compte de Monte-Cristo* by Alexandre Dumas
- *Cyrano de Bergerac* by Edmond Rostand
- *Monsieur Ibrahim et les Fleurs du Coran* by Eric-Emmanuel Schmitt (this book is suggested for more mature learners)
- *L'Étranger* by Albert Camus
- *Plays* by Jean-Baptiste Poquelin (under his stage name, Molière)

# Chapter 7

# Activities for Integrating Culture and Language

- **Label items around the house in the target language.** When speaking about those things, name them in the target language instead of English. Do not write the word in English along with the new language, remember the brain will default to English.
- **Watch movies in the target language without the subtitles!** Start with short clips or shows, such as children's cartoons. Progress to longer shows and films. Animated children's films are an excellent choice for this activity, for all ages.
- **Play games in the target language.** Games like "Memory" and "Bingo" are an excellent way to engage the brain in the new language. Make sure you are matching pictures to words in the target language and not using any type of translation.
- **Listen to music, listen to stories, listen, listen, listen, and then listen some more!** There are lot of excellent language learning podcasts, just be sure they are not using translation. There is also music available on streaming apps like Spotify and Pandora. With the Amazon Echo, you can stream radio stations from all over the world.
- **Give the gift of experiences, not things.** For birthdays and holidays, why not give the gift of experiences instead of things? Children only play with toys for a short time, but memories and education are forever.

  For Christmas and birthdays my children receive a small present from Santa, a book, something to wear, and then a big gift of experience. In past years we have given family travel to different places in the world, ballet lessons, performing arts lessons (choir, acting, etc), small family trips, and tickets to the theater.

Why not give the gift of travel to your children, or the gift of language classes. Enroll them in art classes, or take them to see a play, the symphony, the opera, or the ballet. These are memories that will last a lifetime for your children and for your whole family, plus it gives the opportunity to spend precious time together.

- **Find recipes and cook dishes from around the world.** Choose one night per week to cook a meal from a different country or region in the world. Do some research on the origins of the dish. Is it eaten often? Maybe it is a dish made for a special holiday. Get to know the food traditions in different countries.

- **Celebrate holidays from different countries.** The most basic example is exploring how different countries and regions of the world celebrate Christmas. Find holidays that are celebrated on each of the continents.

- **Research world religions.** Look beyond the Christian world and learn about Hinduism, Islam, Buddhism, Bahai, Jainism, Shinto, or Judaism. There are 4,300 religions around the world.

- **Invite guest speakers into the classroom.** Find people that live in the community and come from another country or culture. Have them share about the different customs practiced in their culture and teach a little of their language.

- **Put on a Culture Fair.** Every year my sons' school puts on a cultural fair and all the different cultures of students in the school are represented. The last three years my family has represented France. The students love the Culture Fair and learn about countries from all over the world and even learn some language and meet real people who come from those countries!

- **Create cultural art projects.** Students love arts and crafts. We create masks for Mardi Gras, djembe drums from Africa out of Styrofoam cups and colored tape, Ghente Cloths from Ghana out of colored construction paper, maracas from Mexico out of paper cups, or Japanese Windsocks. There are so many ideas.

- **Host an exchange student.** There are many companies out there that bring students from other countries to the United States from two weeks up to one full school year. Hosting an exchange student is a great way to introduce your children to different cultures and languages.

- **Integrate foreign words and structures into your conversations.** Going along with the suggestion to label things around the house with words in the target language, start integrating those words into conversation in daily life, focusing on situational context during a specific language focus time. This means that you work on specific words and structures during certain situations during your daily routine. If you are working on food vocabulary, for example, mealtime is a good time to practice this technique. As you progress further in the target language, eliminate the native language, eventually speaking fully in the target language during the language focus time. It is important to remember that this process may take a long time, especially if you do not have formal instruction along with this process. Still, this is a great way to introduce and integrate language into your home and into your life. Let's use the sentence "I would like some milk please," integrating French as an example. Each of these steps take as long as it takes for the foreign words to become engrained in the brain. The natural progression of this would be:
    o Step 1- I would like some lait, s'il vous plait.
    o Step 2- I would like du lait, s'il vous plait
    o Step 3- Je voudrais du lait s'il vous plait

The above example is very simple, but it's a great way to illustrate how to progressively speak more and more in the target language practicing specific vocabulary and structures in situational context. This technique is not translation, but rather a situation in which using the native language as a tool can be helpful in the progression of language fluency. In addition, it is perfectly normal for children learning two languages from birth to mix languages, and in fact, many times adult expatriots will mix their native languages with the language of the country in which they are living. Therefore, this technique is used in all sorts of linguistic situations and makes for a more natural transition from listening to speaking and spontaneous production.

There are many ideas for integrating culture and language into your home and/or classroom. What are some you do already? What are some you would like to try?

# Bibliography

Alladi, S, Bak, T., Surampudi, B., Shailaja, M., Shukla, A., Chaudhuri, J., & Kaul, S. (2013, November 06). Bilingualism delays age at onset of dementia, independent of education and immigration status. Retrieved December 06, 2018, from http://n.neurology.org/content/early/2013/11/06/01.wnl.0000436620.33155.a4

Alliance Française, C. (Ed.). (2018). Le site de ressources FLE du CAVILAM - AF. Retrieved December 09, 2018, from http://www.leplaisirdapprendre.com/

Black M [Black M]. (2016, August 22). *Je Suis Chez Moi* [Video file]. Retrieved from https://www.youtube.com/watch?v=hsOqEhMumaw

Boroditsky, L. [Tedx Talks]. (2018, May 02). *How Language Shapes the Way We Think* [Video file]. Retrieved from https://www.youtube.com/watch?v=RKK7wGAYP6k&t=5s

Bourrelle, J. S. [Tedx Talks]. (2015, July 10). *How Culture Drives Behaviours* [Video file]. Retrieved from https://www.youtube.com/watch?v=l-Yy6poJ2zs

Bray, R. (1946). *Les fables de La Fontaine.* Paris: Nizet.

Brichet, F. (n.d.). Do re mi Languages. Retrieved December 09, 2018, from http://www.doremilanguages.com/

Brown, M. W., & Hurd, C. (2018). *Goodnight Moon.* New York: Harper-Collins.

Camus, A., & Ward, M. (1988). *The stranger: Albert Camus.* Rockland, MA: Wheeler Pub.

Carle, E. (2018). *The very hungry caterpillar.* New York, NY: Philomel Books.

Commission, E. (2012, June). *Europeans and Their Languages*(Rep.). Retrieved 2018, from European Commission website: http://ec.europa.eu/commfrontoffice/publicopinion/archives/ebs/ebs_386_en.pdf

DePaola, T. (n.d.). 26 *Fairmont Avenue.*

Devlin, K. (2015, July 13). Learning a foreign language a 'must' in Europe, not so in America. Retrieved December 09, 2018, from http://www.pewresearch.org/fact-tank/2015/07/13/learning-a-foreign-language-a-must-in-europe-not-so-in-america/

Diamond, C. (2018). Home. Retrieved December 04, 2018, from http://www.charlottediamond.com/

DiOrio, R., & Hill, C. (2009). *What does it mean to be global?* San Francisco, CA: Little Pickle Press.

Duckworth, S. (Director). (2011, January 15). *Je Suis une Pizza* [Video file]. Retrieved December 06, 2018, from https://www.youtube.com/watch?v=wxystpPE1xU

Dumas, A., & Clapham, M. (2017). *The Count of Monte Cristo*. London: Macmillan Collector's Library.

EdChange - Advocating Equity in Schools and Society. (n.d.). Retrieved December 09, 2018, from http://edchange.org/

Evans, H. [TED]. (2016, May 04). *What Does it Mean to be a Global Citizen?* [Video file]. Retrieved from https://www.youtube.com/watch?v=ODLg_00f9BE&t=677s

Friedman, A. (2015, May 11). America's Lacking Language Skills. Retrieved December 05, 2018, from https://www.theatlantic.com/education/archive/2015/05/filling-americas-language-education-potholes/392876/

Gavin, M. (Director). (2014, November 07). *Why Cultural Diversity Matters* [Video file]. Retrieved September 09, 2018, from https://www.youtube.com/watch?v=48RoRi0ddRU

Goscinny, Uderzo, Bell, A., & Hockridge, D. (2004). Asterix. London: Orion.

Henkes, K. (1991). *Chrysanthemum*. New York: Greenwillow Books.

Hergé, Lonsdale-Cooper, L., & Turner, M. R. (2009). *The adventures of Tintin*. New York: Little, Brown Books for Young Readers, a division of Hachette Book Group.

*Invité: Bradley Cooper A Star is Born* [Television broadcast]. (2018, October 02). In Quotidien. Paris: TF1.

Katz, K. (2013). *The colors of us*. Columbus, O.H.: Zaner-Bloser.

Kaufmann, S. (2017). Language Learning | Blog | The Linguist on Language. Retrieved December 06, 2018, from https://blog.thelinguist.com/

Krashen, S. D. (1995). *Principles and practice in second language acquisition*. New-York, NY: Phoenix.

Langlois, S. (2018). Educorock. Retrieved December 09, 2018, from http://www.educorock.com/

Leblanc, M., & Jepson, E. (2016). *Arsene Lupin*. Leicester: Thorpe.

Lowry, L. (2003). *Number the stars*. New York: Scholastic Teaching Resources.

Marian, V., & Stock, A. (2012, October 31). The Cognitive Benefits of Being Bilingual. Retrieved December 04, 2018, from https://www.ncbi.nlm.nih.gov/nlmcatalog/journals

Martin, B., & Carle, E. (2018). *Brown bear, brown bear, what do you see?* London: Puffin Books.

Mason, B. (2016). Beniko Mason's Website. Retrieved December 09, 2018, from http://www.beniko-mason.net/

Mathabane, M. (2015). *Kaffir boy: The true story of a Black youth's coming of age in Apartheid South Africa*. St. Louis, MO: Turtleback Books.

McBratney, S., & Jeram, A. (2012). *Guess How Much I Love You*. Place of publication not identified: Walkers Books Limited.

Merritt, A. (2013, June 19). Why learn a foreign language? Benefits of bilingualism. Retrieved December 04, 2018, from https://www.telegraph.co.uk/education/educationopinion/10126883/Why-learn-a-foreign-language-Benefits-of-bilingualism.html

Monde, T. (Ed.). (2018). Apprendre le français avec TV5MONDE. Retrieved December 09, 2018, from http://apprendre.tv5monde.com/

Monde, T. (Ed.). (2018). Enseigner le français avec TV5MONDE. Retrieved December 09, 2018, from http://enseigner.tv5monde.com/

NYE, N. S. (2000). *HABIBI. S.l.*: PERFECTION LEARNING.

Palacio, R. J. (n.d.). *Wonder*. United Kingdom: Penguin Books.

Pearlman, R., & Kaban, E. (2018). *Pink is for boys*. Philadelphia: RP Kids.

PECS.com - Picture Your Student Learning. (n.d.). Retrieved December 09, 2018, from http://www.pecs.com/

Perkins, M., & Hogan, J. (2008). *Rickshaw girl*. Watertown, MA: Charlesbridge.

Piller, I. (2012, August 05). Multilingual Europe. Retrieved December 09, 2018, from http://www.languageonthemove.com/multilingual-europe/

Pogosyan, M. (2017). When Learning a Foreign Language Metacognitive strategies and practical tips [Web log post]. Retrieved December 10, 2018, from https://www.psychologytoday.com/us/blog/between-cultures/201708/when-learning-foreign-language

Porter, E. M. (2017). *National Board for Professional Teachers Renewal Portfolio* (Unpublished Master's thesis). National Board for Professional Teachers.

Porter, E. M. (2018). Bon Voyage French School – Learn French. Live French. (J. Winslow & M. Page, Eds.). Retrieved December 10, 2018, from http://www.bvwla.com/

Porter, E. M. (2018, October 06). *Language with the Five Senses*. Lecture presented at TEDx Richland in The Uptown Theater, Richland.

Ryan, P. M. (2018). *Esperanza rising*. New York: Scholastic Press.

Saint-Exupery, A. (2018). *Little Prince*. S.l.: Wordsworth Editions.

Schmitt, E., & Grinfas (2004). *Monsieur Ibrahim et les fleurs du Coran*. München: Digital Publishing.

Sempé, J., & Goscinny, R. (2007). *Le petit Nicolas*. Paris: Gallimard.

Tavangar, H. S. (2009). *Growing up global: Raising children to be at home in the world.* New York: Ballantine Books.

Tavangar, H. S., & Mladic-Morales, B. (2014). *The global education toolkit for elementary learners.* Thousand Oaks: Corwin.

*UNESCO Global Citizenship Education Topics and Learning Objectives* [PDF]. (2015). Paris: UNESCO.

Wanjek, C. (2014, June 02). Learning a New Language at Any Age Helps the Brain. Retrieved December 04, 2018, from https://www.livescience.com/46048-learning-new-language-brain.html

Wiesel, E. (2014). *Night, Elie Wiesel.* New York: Spark Publishing

www.ingramcontent.com/pod-product-compliance
Lightning Source LLC
Chambersburg PA
CBHW030510100426
42813CB00002B/418